motorsports

KARTING

Paul Mason

W

FRANKLIN WATTS

First published in 2009
by Franklin Watts

Copyright © Franklin Watts 2009

Franklin Watts
338 Euston Road
London NW1 3BH

Franklin Watts Australia
Level 17/207 Kent Street
Sydney, NSW 2000

Planning and production by
Tall Tree Limited
Editor: Rob Colson
Designer: Jonathan Vipond

Dewey number 796.7'6

ISBN 978 0 7496 8693 2

Printed in China

Franklin Watts is a division of Hachette Children's
Books, an Hachette UK company.
www.hachette.co.uk

Picture credits:
Daniel Beard: 18 top.
Corbis: 9 (Stephanie Maze), 26 (Jerome
Prevost/TempSport), 29clb (Justin Lane/epa) .
Dreamstime.com: 11 (Terry Poche), 12 (Margojh),
15 top (Steve Mann), 15 bottom (Stepunk), 18
bottom, 21 left (Jaggat), 23 (Anna Omelchenko),
25 (Alangh), 27 (Afby71).
Getty Images: 7 bottom (Lluis Gene/AFP), 8
(Fox Photos), 9 bottom (Philip Brown), 21 right
(Mike Cooper/Allsport).
iStockphoto: 6 (Gabriela Schaufelberger),
10–11 and 14 (Gremlin).
Tony Kart: 29tl.
Federica Scarscelli: 29cl.
Robert Smith: 7 top, 13 top and bottom, 17,
22, 24.
Rex Features: 20.
Jake Zellmer: 19.
Public domain: 3 (Jose Pereira/GNU), 16 (Claudio
PlanetKart).

CONTENTS

GET KARTING!

Anyone who has watched kart racing live knows how exciting it is. Tiny machines whizz round the corners, so low that the drivers' bottoms are almost scraping along the ground. Some racers may be as young as eight years old in the UK, or as young as five years old in the USA!

A SIMPLE SPORT

Kart racing is very simple. Racers usually compete on small circuits with lots of tight corners. In the USA, karts also race on oval tracks. The karts are not difficult to drive. A **novice** can buy a second-hand kart for a few hundred pounds.

△ These drivers are waiting at the start of a karting race. They are experienced drivers, racing in one of karting's top classes.

DIFFERENT CLASSES

Karting is divided into different classes. Younger racers use karts with small engines and no **gears**. As they move into higher classes, the karts they drive get more complicated and powerful. In the top class, the karts can go as fast as many high-performance sports cars.

▲ Superkarts have a streamlined shape that helps them move along the track at top speeds.

KARTING INTO THE BIG TIME

The tight, twisty racetracks used for karting develop the skills that a top-class racing driver needs. Most Formula 1 and Indy car racers began their careers in karting. In any kart race, there could be a future Lewis Hamilton or Hélio Castroneves.

▷ Formula 1 driver Fernando Alonso talks to young karters after an exhibition race. One day, these children may be future professional motorsports champions themselves.

EARLY DAYS OF KARTING

Karts are so simple that it's hard to believe no one thought of them until the 1950s. The first ever powered kart was made in 1956. Then, within just a few years, the kart **craze** had spread around the world.

THE FIRST GO-KART

A man named Art Ingels invented the kart (or go-kart, as it was usually called) in California, USA. Ingels apparently made the **chassis** using scrap metal. The engine is said to have come from an old lawnmower.

◁ *Early karts were made out of scrap materials. People of all ages enjoyed the new invention.*

KART CRAZY!

Within three years of Ingels' invention, there were almost 300 different kart manufacturers in the USA alone. The cheap, fun new motorsport spread around the world as the craze continued. In France, for example, the squealing tyres of a kart race were first heard in 1959.

▷ Kart design began to change as the new motorsports craze spread around the world.

A SIMPLE DESIGN

The first karts had no **suspension** and no gears. The engines were almost all motorbike engines, bolted to a simple metal chassis. Wheels, a seat and a steering wheel completed the kart. Today's basic race karts are not very different.

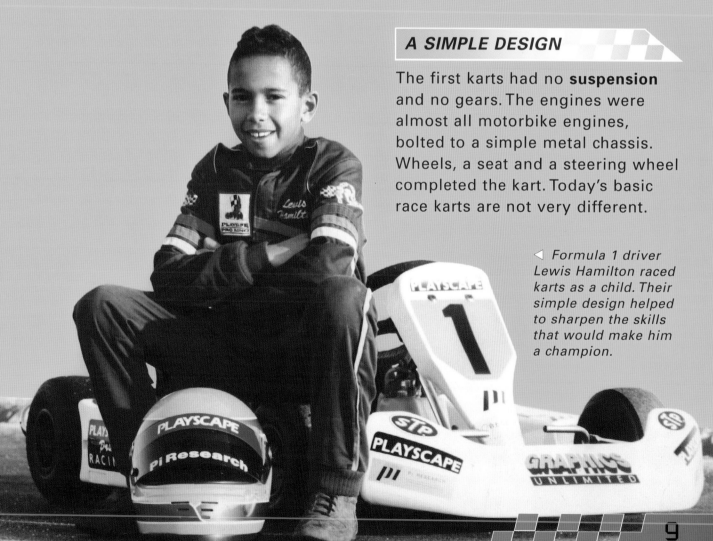

◁ Formula 1 driver Lewis Hamilton raced karts as a child. Their simple design helped to sharpen the skills that would make him a champion.

THE CHASSIS

A kart's chassis is the framework that the engine, wheels and seat are attached to. You might think that the chassis of a vehicle travelling at over 200 kph would be a miracle of engineering – but you wouldn't necessarily be right.

BASIC CHASSIS

A basic kart chassis is a very simple structure, made of steel pipes with attachment points. The parts of the kart, including the engine, are welded to these points. Karts don't have suspension, so the chassis has to **flex** to absorb bumps.

TECHNICAL DATA

Karts don't have a **differential** – a device that allows the rear wheels to go round at different speeds. Because of this, whenever they go round a corner, one wheel skids or rises off the ground.

△ International championship karts feature a straight, open chassis. The seat is in the middle and there is no roll-bar (see opposite) to protect the driver in a crash.

Engine

Steering wheel

Brake pedal

Throttle pedal

TYPES OF CHASSIS

Most race karts drive a 'straight' chassis, with the driver sitting in the middle. In oval racing, where the karts only turn one way, an 'offset' chassis is used. The driver sits to one side, balancing the cornering forces.

▷ *This racer is driving a kart with an offset, closed chassis. A closed chassis has a roll-bar that protects the driver if the car rolls over.*

Roll-bar

THE ENGINE

In the early days of karting, people used all kinds of engines to power their machines. Motors were taken from lawnmowers, motorbikes and chainsaws – people would use any engine small enough to fit behind the driver's seat. Today, things are very different.

MODERN ENGINES

A kart weighs about the same as a grown man – just one tenth of the weight of a family car. Although karts are light, their engines are extremely powerful. A kart engine can now generate as much power as some cars. It's no wonder karts are so exciting to drive!

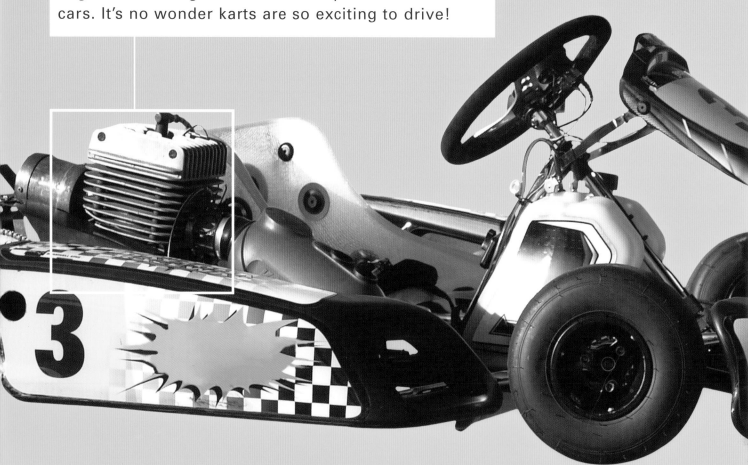

△ *Before the race starts, every detail of the kart is checked to make sure the driver has the best chance of winning – and of safely reaching the finish.*

▽ *In an 'offset' kart, the engine is mounted to one side of the driver, instead of at the back. This puts the driver's weight to the left-hand side, giving the kart extra cornering* **grip**.

ENGINE CLASSES

Different types of engines are used for different racing classes. In general, younger, lighter racers use less powerful engines. Older, heavier, more experienced racers get to use the really powerful engines.

International races use three different types of engine, depending on the category of race:

- KF-class karts use a 125cc (cubic centimetre) engine with no gears.
- KZ-class karts use 125cc engines with gears.
- Superkarts use 250cc engines with gears.

△ *Most karts don't have gears, but 'shifter karts' like these ones do. Shifter karts are used in top-level racing classes.*

TECHNICAL DATA

The most powerful race karts can accelerate to 100 kph in less than three seconds. They have good grip, too – the sideways pull the drivers feel as they whizz round corners can be three times as powerful as the force of gravity!

TUNING THE KART

At any small kart race, there are usually a couple of worried-looking parents rooting through a toolkit, looking for a missing spanner. Although karts are simple machines, a lot can be done to tune them for a race.

TECHNICAL DATA

*Karts use **carburettors**, or 'carbs', to blend the fuel with air before it enters the engine, instead of computer-controlled fuel injection like most cars. Setting up the carbs to work as well as possible is crucial if you want to win races.*

ACCELERATION AND SPEED

Most non-geared kart engines power the rear wheel using a chain and cogs, like the wheel of a bicycle. Changing the size of the cogs affects acceleration and top speed, just like changing gear on a bike.

Drivers change the cogs depending on whether they need high top speed or fast acceleration.

- Fewer teeth on the rear cog and more on the front gives a high top speed, but slower acceleration.

- More teeth on the rear cog and fewer on the front gives a faster acceleration, but lower top speed.

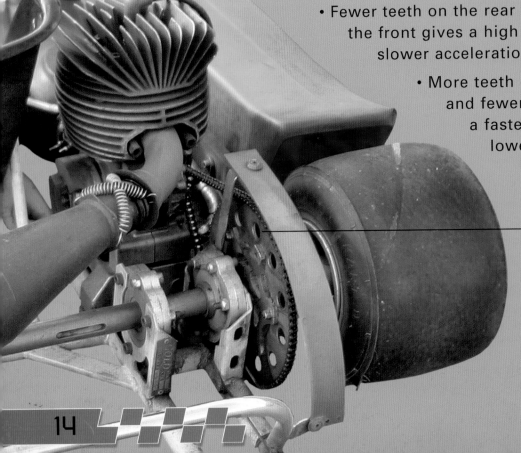

Chain and cogs attached to rear wheel

◁ *Non-geared karts use different combinations of cogs to alter the speed and acceleration of the vehicle.*

TYRES

Tyre choice also gives kart racers the chance to tune their vehicle. Depending on the weather, they can choose tyres to suit dry, wet and in-between (or **intermediate**) conditions. For racing on slippery dirt or clay surfaces, kart drivers cut grooves into slick dry-weather tyres. There are even spiked tyres for racing on ice.

▷ *Smooth, slick tyres are used in dry-weather races. They give maximum grip, and unlike wet-weather tyres, they don't need grooves that will carry away water.*

ADJUSTING THE CHASSIS

The amount of flex in a kart chassis sometimes needs to be changed. On a smoother track, there is less need to absorb bumps. In which case, some drivers add stiffening rods to the chassis to make it less flexible.

△ *Drivers set up their karts to get the best possible speed out of the engine, chassis and tyres.*

SPRINT RACING

Welcome to the fast and furious side of kart racing: the sprint race! The all-action thrills, spills, slides and crashes of sprint racing make it exciting for racers and spectators alike.

SHORT RACES

Sprint races don't last very long. The drivers take no more than 15 minutes to finish a small number of laps. Normally, three of these short races decide which drivers make it into the final, with a chance to get on the podium.

SPRINT CIRCUITS

Sprint racetracks are like smaller versions of the tracks that Formula 1 drivers race on. They feature tight bends with **kerbs** to bump the kart off; long, sweeping curves; and straight sections for building up overtaking speed.

▶ In a sprint race, drivers have just a few laps to prove their skills at handling sweeping curves and tight bends.

KARTING WORLD CHAMPIONSHIP

The biggest competition in sprint racing is the annual Karting World Championship. The racers drive 125cc karts with the **revs** limited to 16,000 **rpm**. The karts are earsplittingly loud, especially when ten go racing past you together on the straight!

△ *Young drivers jostle for position at the start of a sprint race. The smoke from kart 41 is due to a wheel locking because of hard braking.*

SPEEDWAY KARTING

Speedway kart races happen on dirt- or clay-surface oval tracks. The lumps, bumps and slides that these tracks provide make for exciting racing. Some of the karts even have a roll-bar to protect the driver.

RACETRACKS

Speedway kart tracks are usually made up of two long left-hand bends and two straights. One of the long bends is sometimes tighter than the other. From above, these tracks can look like the shape of a stretched-out egg.

▽ *These speedway karts have roll-bars to protect their driver if they flip over.*

QUALIFYING AND RACING

There are two types of qualifying for speedway races:

• The drivers do a timed lap. The fastest drivers get into the main race, which usually lasts for 20 laps.

• The best drivers from two short qualifying races get into the main race.

LEFT TURN ONLY

Speedway racers travel in one direction round the track, so they only ever turn left! Their karts sometimes have the seat on the left-hand side. The driver's weight presses down harder on that side, giving a bit more grip during turns.

◁ *Dust flies up from the dirt track as the drivers race through a corner during a speedway race.*

TECHNICAL DATA

*Speedway **ovals** are quite small. They are rarely more than 400 metres long – the same distance as most running tracks!*

ENDURANCE RACES

Most kart races last about 15 minutes, but endurance races (enduros) are much longer. The winner is whoever does the most laps in a set time. Some last 24 hours – which makes it impossible for one driver to be at the wheel for the whole race!

TRACK AND RACE LENGTH

Endurance races usually take place on a full-size car-racing track. These are generally between 2.4 and 6.4 kilometres long. The races often last up to an hour, with one driver per kart and no pit stops.

▽ *Enduro racing is fun, even in the mud! These knobbly, grippy tyres help the racers to handle the track.*

LONGER RACES

The longest endurance races last for 24 hours or more. They have at least two drivers per kart, with one resting while the other drives. Each kart has a **pit crew**. This is a team of people who do refuelling, tyre changes and repairs.

△ A driver drifts and corrects his steering during a race in Malaysia. Even a slight lapse in concentration could lead to a skid or an accident.

LE MANS 24-HOUR RACE

Le Mans, France, hosts the world's most famous kart race: the Le Mans 24-Hour. The drivers race through the night under floodlights, in almost any weather. In 2008, the race was suspended for the first time ever. A violent storm at 4 am made it impossible to drive.

▷ During an endurance race, drivers need to be able to complete laps quickly, while maintaining their level of concentration over a long period of time.

TECHNICAL DATA

The Le Mans 24-Hour kart race features the famous 'Le Mans start'. When the start signal goes, the drivers run across the track to their karts before racing off with a screech of tyres.

SUPPORT CREW

At small, local kart races, the support crew is often made up of a young driver's relatives. They have towed the kart to the track and helped to get it ready for racing. At big races, however, it's a different story.

PRODUCING A WINNING KART

The biggest kart teams can spend lots of money on producing a winning kart. They design the chassis, analyse how engines work on different fuel settings and have access to the best tyres. They also have more opportunities to test their karts before racing.

▽ At big races, the support crew are a team of experts who keep the kart and the driver in top condition.

RACE-DAY HELP

Drivers for bigger kart teams get help on race day, so they can focus more of their attention on winning. Their support crew includes a team of mechanics helps with changes to the engine, chassis, tyres and other tuning.

▲ A team manager holds out a pit board for his driver. The pit board gives the driver information, such as his or her position in the race or when to refuel.

TECHNICAL DATA

Sometimes, one kart design works so well that it is used widely. In 2007, for example, Tony Kart/Vortex were almost impossible to beat in the Karting World Championship. By 2008, however, other designs had caught up and the racing was as close as ever!

FITNESS AND TRAINING

Successful kart drivers have to be fit. As Jack Hawksworth, a top kart driver, says: 'When you're not fit enough you lose valuable tenths [of a second] at the end of the race... your concentration can wander and you begin to make mistakes.'

RACE SAFETY

Karting was originally quite dangerous – not only for the racer but also for the support crew! Early karts had to be pushed to get them going. The pusher was left standing on the track, with other karts whizzing past. Today's safety regulations have made karting much safer.

TRACK SAFETY

During a race, safety marshals with fire extinguishers stand by and ambulances are ready to speed into action if there is an accident. **Scrutineers** check every kart to make sure it is safe to drive.

▽ *These marshals are helping to clear a broken-down kart from the race track to avoid an accident.*

◁ *This yellow flag warns drivers to slow down to avoid an obstacle ahead.*

TECHNICAL DATA

FLAGS

If there is a problem during a race, flags are waved to tell the drivers what is happening:

• *Red flag at start line: race stopped.*

• *Black flag (sometimes with orange dot): kart must pull in.*

• *Black-and-white flag: warning for unsporting behaviour.*

• *Yellow flag: slow down and do not overtake – there is a hazard ahead.*

• *Yellow flag with red stripes: oil or water on track means less grip ahead.*

• *Green flag: track clear ahead.*

• *Blue flag: you are about to be overtaken by a faster kart.*

MODERN SAFETY GEAR

Every driver wears a full-face helmet to protect their face and eyes. Many drivers also wear HANS (head and neck support) devices while racing. These lightweight frames are designed to prevent neck injuries. Drivers also wear fireproof clothing, including gloves. Special shoes prevent their feet being crushed or burned in an accident.

MOVING ON

Karting isn't just a great motorsport, it is also a stepping-stone to a career in other motorsports. A few kart racers have gone on to earn millions of pounds driving top-level racing cars or motorbikes.

TECHNICAL DATA

*Many people think the Brazilian Formula 1 driver Ayrton Senna (born 21 March 1960, died 1 May 1994) was one of the best racing drivers ever. Senna used to say that karting was a perfect **breeding ground** for race drivers. Mind you, he would say that: he won his first ever kart race at just 13!*

TRAINING FOR THE TOP

Karting provides great training for racing more powerful cars. Kart drivers learn how changes in speed and direction affect a four-wheeled vehicle. They see how far they can push the tyres before losing grip, and they look at the tactics that successful racers need.

▽ *Ayrton Senna at the wheel of his kart. He was a world champion who sharpened his driving skills at a young age by competing in kart races.*

STAR DRIVERS FROM KARTING

Most of the world's top racing drivers started behind the steering wheel of a kart. Among them are:

• Seven-times Formula 1 world champion Michael Schumacher.

• 2005 and 2006 Formula 1 champion Fernando Alonso.

• 2008 Formula 1 champion Lewis Hamilton.

Many Indy car and Nascar racers also began their racing careers in karting, including Dan Wheldon, Lake Speed, Juan Pablo Montoya and Ricky Rudd. Even motorcycle racers have dabbled in karting, such as six-times MotoGP champion Valentino Rossi.

△ The front wheel of Lewis Hamilton's car lifts off the ground as it turns a corner during a Formula 1 Grand Prix – a skill that Hamilton would have learnt during his early years of kart racing.

GLOSSARY

breeding ground
Place where young animals start their lives, but in this sense it describes a place where new talents – such as driving skills – are developed.

carburettors
Mechanical devices that mix fuel with air to power an engine.

chassis
Framework to which all the other parts of a vehicle are attached.

craze
Activity or way of doing something that becomes popular very quickly.

differential
Device to allow the rear wheels of a vehicle to go round at different speeds. Differentials help vehicles turn corners.

flex
A good kart chassis has to flex (or bend) in exactly the right way for both cornering and speed.

gear
Disc or wheel with teeth (grooves) on the outside edge. Gears allow power to be transmitted from an engine to the wheels. Different sizes allow different speeds.

grip
Amount of attachment or stickiness a tyre has on the racetrack.

intermediate
In racing, intermediate (in-between) tyres are used when the weather is mixed or in-between dry and wet weather.

kerbs
Raised edges to a track or road that racing drivers can use to corner.

novice
A novice driver is a beginner.

ovals
Racetracks that are mostly oval in shape. Many 'ovals' are actually more egg-shaped than oval.

pit crew
Team of people who wait in a special area (called the pits) to help the driver with maintenance or other problems.

rev
Short for 'revolution', which describes one turn of an engine's drive wheel.

rpm
Short for 'revs per minute', a measurement of an engine's speed.

scrutineers
Officials at racetracks who examine vehicles to make sure they are within the regulations and safe to drive.

suspension
Mechanical device or devices that absorb bumps as a vehicle moves on a surface.

STAR DRIVERS

MARCO ARDIGÒ

Born: 26 June 1983
Nationality: Italian

Ardigò won the Karting World Championship in 2007. He won again in 2008, proving himself to be one of the top modern kart racers.

DAVIDE FORÉ

Born: 16 July 1974
Nationality: Italian

Four-times world karting champion (1998, 2000, 2004 and 2006), Foré is the leading modern kart racer. He first raced a kart when he was eight years old.

FRANÇOIS GOLDSTEIN

Nationality: Belgian

In the late 1960s and early 1970s, Goldstein dominated kart racing, winning the World Championship five times. He was famous for his aggressive driving style.

LEWIS HAMILTON

Born: 7 January 1985
Nationality: British

Hamilton was a British and European junior champion in kart racing before he won the Formula 1 World Championship in 2008.

DAN WHELDON

Born: 22 June 1978
Nationality: British

Wheldon started his racing career in karts, but now earns his living driving in the Indy car series. In 2005, he won the Indy car championship.

WEBSITES

www.karting1.co.uk
A magazine-style website with the latest karting news, as well as technical advice and interviews with leading racers.

www.youtube.com
Go to YouTube and key in, 'karting, helmet cam.' Ladies and gentlemen, fasten your seatbelts and get ready for a thrilling ride!

www.cikfia.com
The CIK (Commission Internationale de Karting) is the international governing body for kart racing.

www.karting.co.uk
This website aims to provide comprehensive information on karting in the UK. You can find out technical tips on tuning a kart, advice from top drivers, news about racing, a directory of kart tracks, information about classes and much more.

www.goingkarting.co.uk
A website useful to anyone interested in karting, with handy articles on topics ranging from getting started in karting to building your own kart, fitness régimes for budding stars and safety advice.

INDEX